Success Mantras Given By Leonardo da Vinci

(1st book of Leonardo da Vinci Series)

Uttam Kr. Ghosh

Published by

WC Publisher

The characters and events portrayed in this book are Non-fictitious. Content written in this book is not intended to harm or insult any sentiments of any person, religion, cast, gender, etc.

ISBN-10: 8712963768
ISBN-13: 9798712963768

Cover design by: Gulam Mustafa Raza
Publishers: WC Publishers

Thank You

Late Jiwan Ghosh who gave me knowledge about this great Genius in my childhood. That inspiration inspired me to know more about Leonardo.

I want to thank my mother who is with me in my rise and fall.

I want to thank my all friends for being always with me. I thank Firoz Ahemad, Syed Azhar Imam, Gautam Singh, Tribhuwan Nath Gautam, Mukesh, Pushpendra Shankar Pandey, Komal Singh, Anubhav Srivastava, and many others.

Every man is solely responsible for not getting success in his life- Uttam Kr. Ghosh

Index

Preface..6

Part One

His Life..9
His Characters 21

Part Two

Success Mantras of Leonardo da Vinci........................25
Correct your thoughts..25
Never Forget the sense of Curiosity............................27
Ready to Learn...31
Be Ready to Accept Your Faults..................................32
Make Lists..36
Most Important Mantra – Do Your Action.................38
Never Feel Distressed...43
Organized Manner of Doing Action............................45
The Fear of What If We Fail..46

Part Three

Some Works of Leonardo da Vinci..............................50
In Paintings (Mona Lisa)..50
In Science...55
In Geology..59
On the Flights of Birds...61

Preface

Many of us wants to know if there is anyone who is an expert in many fields. If you Google, you will get only one name – Leonardo da Vinci. He is also known as a genius. You can ask me why. The answer is quite simple. He was an expert on so many things. You can find him best in so many aspects. We will know some of them in this book.

Many of us know him as the creator of the most mysterious painting **Mona Lisa** or the great painting **The Last Supper**. The most expensive painting ever sold is "**Salvador Mundi**" which is sold at the price of $ 450.3 million. It is bought by Crown Prince Mohammad Bin Salman. It was due to appear at the Louvre Museum in Abu Dhabi.

But ....but.....but.....he was not only one of the greatest painters of all the time. He was an astronomer, anatomist, scientist, mathematician, musician, engineer, etc., etc. has a lot remaining.

Surprised!!!

How can a man be an expert on so many things? We will get an answer to this **how** in this book.

But we are so smart people that we'll ask for sure, "What is my benefit in knowing about him?"

In this book, you will get the way to be successful as there are **success mantras given by the most genius person of all time- Leonardo da Vinci.**

So ready????

His Life

Early Life (1452-1467)

The day of 15th April 1452 was a normal day but not a normal one yet. This day is the witness of a new era in the history of humans. The most genius or the most mysterious person in many fields – Leonardo da Vinci born on the earth exactly at Via de Anchiano, a town located 3 km north of Vinci, Republic of Florence(Italy). His father Ser Piero da Vinci was a well-established notary (a kind of solicitor who drafted and interpreted legal documents) and a landlord of the town. His father never married his mother Caterina di MeoLippi. She was a peasant and orphan. He lived five years of his early age with his mother thereafter settled with his father.

He would however write letters to his mother from time to time. His grandfather was very happy at his birth. He wrote in his diary, "A grandson born in-home on Saturday, April 15, 1452, at 10:30 of night. He is the son of Ser."

Leonardo had no surname. The meaning of Leonardo da Vinci is Leonardo of Vinci. Actually, his family used the Vinci city name as a surname. Fortunately, Leonardo was treated as a legitimate son. His father was most often out of the city due to his work. So Leonardo was not so fortunate to feel the love of his parents. Did it make him depressed?

No.............not at all.

Leonardo's Home in his Village. Public Domain

His uncle looked after him as well as the business of home and property. Leonardo used to go everywhere with his uncle. Usually, he always had a notebook or sketchbook with him. He used to sit anywhere near nature and started observing each and everything he could see. Anything which he liked most, became a part of his sketchbook. He was aware of the power of notes and images from his very early age.

His very first known Sketch made in his childhood. Credit: Public domain

At the age of four, he had witnessed a very strong storm that passed near to his town. The storm destroyed everything of his way. He was amazed by the power of nature. This made him closer to nature.

Like all other boys, he also received the traditional elementary education. He was not so good in Latin and mathematics. Latin was the key language of his time. It was in his later age when he took Latin and mathematics seriously. At his initial age, he was not a good student but his teachers were aware of his talent.

Once his math teacher, being tired of his questions, told him, "I can't teach you more Leonardo, I taught you everything I know."

He was so talented that in a short span of time, he learned to play a musical instrument 'Lyre'. He started singing and composing. Once his music teacher said, " I never listen so much soothing music and voice".

In this time period, we can see that he was a very curious, self-dependent mind, very talented, and lover of nature. This period shows his early interest in the surroundings and as an artist, musician and sketcher. This period had a wonderful seed that germinated in the bright future of our genius- Leonardo da Vinci.

1467-1481

Leonardo's artistic inclinations were caught by his father and he sent him to the famous artist of that time Andrea del Verrocchio at the age of 14. Verrocchio was considered perhaps the greatest artist living in Florence. At present, he is remembered as one of the leading painters from the early Renaissance. He worked as an apprentice. That was a pretty good place to unfold his multitalented personality. During this six-year period, he learned many different techniques and developed many technical skills. He learned metalworking, working with leather, the arts, carving, sculpting, and of course drawing and painting. He also worked in the workshop of artist Antonio. By the age of 20, he had become a master craftsman of the guild and opened his own studio.

In 1472 he is accepted into the painter's guild of Florence, but he remained with Verrochio for 5 more years. According to Giorgio Vasari, who wrote Leonardo's biography in his book 'From Lives of the Most Excellent Painters', when Verrochio saw a painting made by Leonardo, become so much overwhelmed that he left painting from that day. However, most scholars dismiss Vasari's account as apocryphal.

It is thought that Verrochio completed his work "Baptism of Christ" around 1475 with the help of Leonardo, who painted part of the background and the young angel holding the robe of Jesus. In 1478, Leonardo left his studio and opened his own studio.

After opening his studio, he received his first independent commission for an art piece that had to place inside of Florence's Palazzo Vecchio. In 1481 Augustinian monks of Florence's San Donato a Scopeto gave him the task of painting 'Adoration of the Magi'.

Leonardo left the city and abandon both the projects without ever completing them. Why??

It is very surprising that one young artist who just received two very nice commissions left the city. This indicates that he had some deeper reasons to leave Florence. He had an experience-oriented scientific mind and had no competition in Florence and Milan was a much better place according to him. This decision was certainly recommended by Lorenzo the Magnificent, due to some diplomatic reasons. Medici encouraged artists of Florence to travel to the courts of other Italian princes.

Leonardo wanted to serve in the court of Duke Ludovico Sforza. So he left Florence.

This period is known for its mechanical designs and of human figures.

Leonardo had to give his biodata to the duke. It is a very surprising factor for us. Here you can see the image of his original biodata. I know you cannot read what is written in the image. So I am giving some points of it here.

Some Points of Leonardo's biodata

1. I have some concepts to make light but strong bridges that can be carried very easily.
2. I know how in seize of land, removing water from the ditches and doing an infinite number of bridges, rope stairs and other tools.
3. If for the height of the ground or for the strength of the place and the site you couldn't use the bomb siege in a siege, I know ways to end up with citadels and fortresses, even when they are built on the rock.
4. I also have the ideas for making canons that are very comfortable and very easy to transfer, to throw stones as small as hail rain.
5. I can also make tanks, safe and harmless to enter enemy lines with artillery, and they won't be any company of men in arms so big that can get rid of the tanks. And after them the infantry will arrive and find them practically unarmed and opposition.(here he was talking about modern tanks.)
6. In peaceful times, I believe that I can give as much satisfaction as any other in architecture, in building public and private buildings, as well as in driving water from one place to another.
7. I can make marble, bronze or mud sculptures, as well as paintings, and my work can compare

to anyone else's, whoever it is. (You can see his self confidence and belief in himself).

It can be seen clearly here that he was offering his service as an engineer, an architect, a painter and a sculpture.

1481-99

He was appointed in the court of duke Ludovici Sforza in Milan. His great art and genius approach gave more and more regard to the court. Leonardo was also consulted for the works of architecture, engineering, and military matters. He was listed as 'picter di ingenlarius du Calis' means painter and engineer of the Duke, in the register of the royal households.

During this period Leonardo was given a grand task which would be the main reason, he was invited to Milan. It was a monumental equestrian statue in bronze to be erected in honour of Francesco Sforza, the founder of the Sforza dynasty. Leonardo devoted 12 years to this task. In 1493, the clay model of the horse was put on public display on the occasion of the marriage of Emperor Maxililian to Bianca Maria Sforza. It was 16 feet high. However, he was unable to finish the task. The reasons were out of control. Italy was invaded by France. The metal collected for the purpose of making the monument was used to make cannons to be used in the war.

Despite this failure, this period of 17 years is known for the completion of his most famous painting like 'The Last Supper' and 'The Virgin of The Rocks'.

1500-1508

In 1500 he returned to Florence to pursue projects in paintings, anatomy, and engineering. In 1503, he was commissioned to paint a mural in Florence's Palazzo Vacchio; it was to be a grand historical scene intended to glorify the military conquest of the Florentines. Again this work was never completed, however, 1503 was the year when he began the most famous and the most mysterious painting- Mona Lisa. He was never satisfied with the painting and edited it again and again but never completed it.

1508-1513

This period is known as the era of science. He dedicated himself to an extensive study of human anatomy. He dissected bodies more than any doctor of that age. In addition, he also persuaded mathematics, geological, optical and botanical studies.

1513-1516

Leonardo left Italy to serve king Francis I of France. He did little in paintings in the period but continued to pursue the study of anatomy and to draw powerful natural events. He spent the last three years of life in a small residence of Cloux near the king's summer palace at Ambiose on the Loire. He was given the title of Premier peintre, architecte et mechancien du Roi (first painter, architect, and engineer of the king).

May 2, 1519

Unfortunately, the day came when he died. He died in Cloux (now clasluce), France, and was buried at the church of Saint Florentin. When the French revolution arrived at the beginning of 1900, the church was torn down. The whereabouts of Leonardo's remains are no longer known. his grave can no longer be located.

His Character

Undoubtedly he was a great gentleman. He was always in his thoughts most of the time. His early biographers described him as a man with great personal appeal, kindness, and generosity. He was generally well-loved by his contemporaries except for a few ones. According to Vasari, "Leonardo's disposition was so lovable that he commanded everyone's affection."

As Vasari said, "His magnificent presence brought comfort to the most trouble soul; he was so persuasive that he could bend other people to his will..... He was so generous that he fed all his friends rich or poorer..... Through his birth, Florence received a very great gift, and through his death, it sustained an incalculable loss. Vasari said at one place' "in the normal course of events many men and women are born with various remarkable qualities and talents; but occasionally, in a way that transcends nature, a single person is marvelously endowed by heaven with beauty, grace, and talent in such abundance that he leaves other men far behind......

He died due to a stroke possibly. According to Vasari, from the book Lives of the painters, the king raised him and lifted his head to help him. He passed away at the moment in the king's arms. Many researchers believed this story as a legendry rather than a fact. He died but became immortal by his so many great works. He was a perfect example of how to be great without taking too much pressure in life. The only object of life should be to live great and to die never to die. I collected and refine all his thoughts which can help us to be successful in our life. Let's come and search for ourselves.

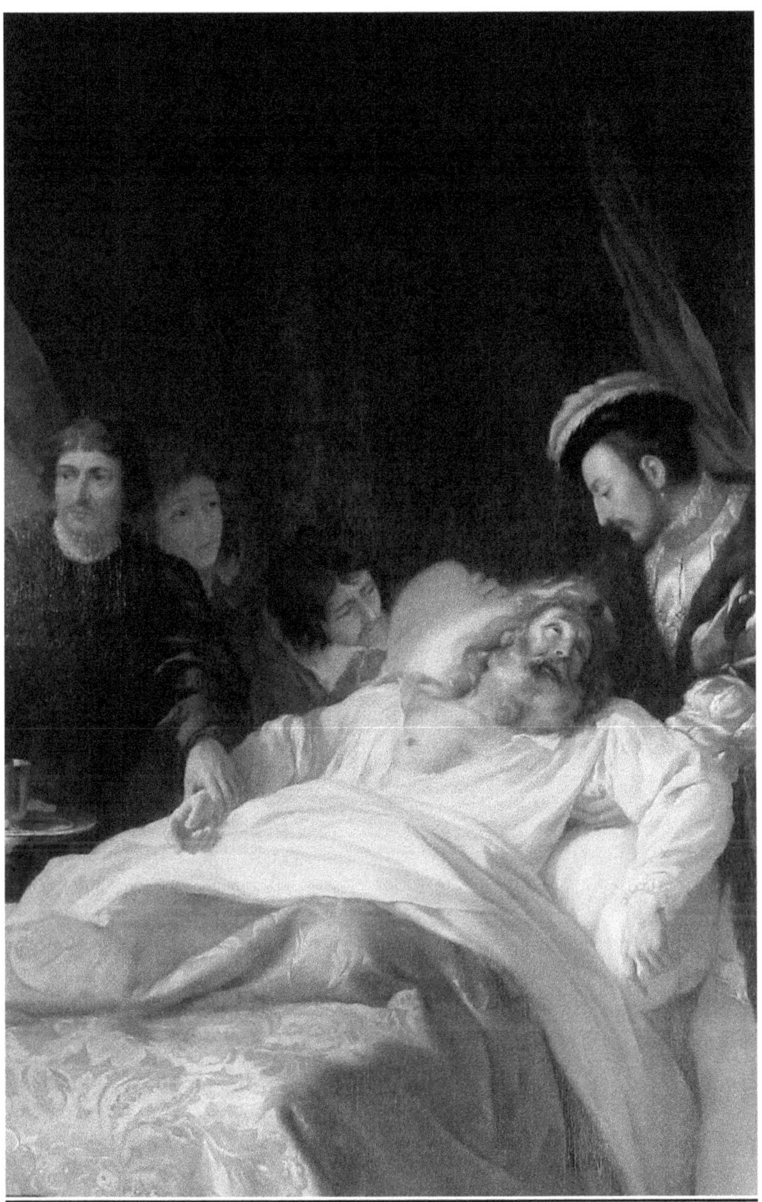

Part Two

Success Mantras of Leonardo da Vinci

Leonardo wrote and lived many secrets of success from time to time. Not only in his writing but in his actions, he showed us the true path of achieving our goals and being successful in our one and only life. Here you not only can read them but also can make plans and organize yourself. These steps are so much proven that it is not possible that you follow them but fail. Always remember there is a success path designed for you only.

Come and rediscover yourself...........

Correct Your Thoughts

The greatest deception man suffer is from their own opinions. – Leonardo da Vinci

It is the very first step. I want you to stop reading, close your eyes and think about your failures. Give here some minutes to your subconscious mind in search of the deepest roots of the reasons, why you fail. Do it...........

Please!!!

Now tell yourself what reasons do you find. The reason is only you except for one or two cases. The circumstances could be worst but that is not the cause. The reason is only you, who lost courage when life demanded it most from you.

Everyone in us is unique in true manners. You have at least one talent or quality best in the world. We are busy searching for what is happening in the world but fail to understand what is in trouble within us. There is not a single person, not only in the world but also in the universe, who makes you fail. It is only you, you, and only you.

To accept this is the first step to throw all the garbage from your mind. Make yourself ready for a long fight, fight to get yourself what you deserve. How??

Let's search our own success path on the following pages.

Never Forget Sense of Curiosity

Be curious. Yes, be curious about everything you can see around you. Actually, it's a basic low of getting success. Even Elbert Einstein said once, "I am not intelligent, but curious. Want to know how things work."

Being curious, Leonardo got deep knowledge and became a truly universal man- a man who was a master of so many fields. Once he was curious about the flight of birds. He started to watch birds and their activities carefully. To know more in detail, he started dissected birds' bodies. This curiosity made history. He was the first who gave an accurate theory of birds' flight in his book 'Codex on the Flight of Birds'. He understood the laws of aerodynamics. I told you somewhere in the book that he made many designs of flying machines. His one design is just like today's helicopter and one like an airplane. He also made a design of a parachute.

How was he able to design such things which came into existence so much later of his time? You will find just one answer........curiosity.

Just let me talk about ourselves. At which frame of age, did we learn the most in our lives? In school, in college, or any university? No! we learn most in our childhood. We are able to learn so many things just due to our childhood curiosity. Curiosity is good. Right ?? if the answer is yes, why do we leave this habit when we became wiser? Leave reading here for a while and just think about it.

I think we all have the same answer that we know everything beneficial for us in this money-centered world. Oh! Really ? is actually we know ?? if you ask any wise person, he will say that be a master of your own field and we have to choose the field of our interest. I want to discover, how many of us are in the field we dreamt for? If I ask you the reason why did you not choose that field of your interest? why we were not working in the field which could give us more joy and satisfaction?

There are hundreds of reasons for not choosing the field of our interest. But there are only two reasons, you have to think again. First, you are not satisfied actually in our life in which we live only to fulfill the needs of living. But ask yourself, to live like a machine is good for you or you want something else. The second reason is satisfaction. If you like singing, just leave everything and sing a song for yourself and then tell me what did you feel. Satisfaction...Interest is not a thing my dear to be forgotten. How will we be an expert of our field? curiosity to know each and every how and why of your field.

I start believing in this law of curiosity. My father was the first who told me about this larger-than-life type of man. What he told me, made me more curious to know about Leonardo da Vinci. I digested many books about him but this many was very little to understand a person like him. The pressure of scoring good in my academics and my liking for mathematics killed my curiosity about Leonardo. Fortunately, sometimes ago my curiosity took rebirth. I started to know and think about him again. What was the result? The result is in the form of a book you are reading at the very moment. And me it is a matter of ultimate satisfaction that you are reading my book.

Being curious is necessary for success. I understand that we can't be curious at the level of Leonardo. He crossed the limits. Once he was curious about how the muscles of the human face work. Any mishandling of dead bodies was a serious offense at the time of Vinci. The punishment for this crime was death penalty but he preferred his curiosity. He started visiting graveyards, digging graves, and getting dead bodies. He started dissection of bodies and as the result, he was the first who gave each and every detailing of human anatomy. Actually, he would be the father of human anatomy but unfortunately, we got those notebooks later in 1965.

So I am not telling you to be curious beyond a limit but to be curious about your field, about your subjects, and about anything. Do act to feed the hunger of your curiosity and your nose will sense the smell of success.

Ready to learn

Learning never exhausts the mind- Leonardo da Vinci

Always ready to learn new things. Do you know the importance of that? Do remember, just sometime before, audio and video cassettes were very popular. No one, except one, thought that they could be replaced by anything else. Yes except one, who thought about the future and used the new inventions of science and as a result gave us memory chips or cards. The bigger and hard to handle ones were replaced by smaller ones. Now we can't imagine life without memory cards but one day more compact and more efficient device will replace them too.

You have to learn new things, to adopt new techniques and ideas in your field, whatever your field is.

Leonardo used oil paints in his paintings at a time when no one was aware of their uses. Normally if anyone wants to be a painter, he starts to learn the techniques of sketching and painting but what Leonardo did? He started to learn the mechanism of the human eye. He learned how the human eye looks or watches anything. He started using in making his paintings the lessons that he learned. And as the result, he started to make three-dimensional paintings. Believe me or not, it was magic at that time. People couldn't believe at first sight, what they had seen. Many researchers are researching his painting techniques.

Actually, his thinking process was ahead of his age. He thought of new things and started employing them in his works, and you know what the results are. So, learn new things and techniques and do start practicing them, and make yourself the center of appreciation.

Be Ready to Accept Your Own Faults

Yes, it is very important to learn about our own faults. Here our ego plays a vital role. It is difficult to conscience it that we are human and we can do mistakes. Let us learn this art from the genius, Leonardo. He was a great painter of his time too. It was possible that his ego would be big. But no....

He was aware that he could be wrong. His great piece of art 'Mona Lisa' is a true identity of him for us. Many of us know his name as a painter of this painting. But do you know this painting is not complete? He took years and years to edit his own work but was never satisfied with his own work. Actually, he never gave it to the person who gave him the work of making it as according to him it was not completed. What do we do in our daily life? We got work and complete it in a little time whether it is nicely done or not. We are in a hurry as we have lots of work. As the result, our no work is called extraordinary. There are many painters who made many paintings in a short span of time and earn a little and on the opposite, there are some painters who made one painting in a long time but earn a huge amount. What is better? who will you choose to make a painting of our loved ones?

I want to say that our thinking of 'it's ok' makes our thought and work limited. If you want to succeed, you have to think beyond the limits. When we learn to accept our faults, not in front of anybody else but in front of ourselves, we will able to achieve greater things. Remember, it is sure that there is something special and unique within you. You have to discover yourself, you have to polish yourself and you will see the magic. You can choose to live ordinary or to change yourself a little and live extraordinarily. The choice is only yours.

Most of us make us limited in daily routine. If someone asks you about the best thing you could do in past, it will make you uncomfortable. Your most probable answer will be just like, "leave this topic. I have no time". Or "earning is more important than fulfilling my dreams or interest." I know a lot of people who sing well or dance well or can do sketching well. At their age, they have dreams like being a great one in their fields of interest. I know you, yes, you, who is reading this line also dreamt to achieve something but why did you not do that? O! you were unable to do so due to the pressure of education or earning, right? Now tell me one thing. Was actually there no time for your interest? I can take guarantee that you had the time. Actually, it was you who killed your dreams. You are the killer of yourself or maybe of a great artist or a great scientist. You have a lot of time yes. It is not too late and you have a lot of time but for that. Yes but for that, you have to leave watching online useless videos, or limit your time on social platforms, or leave your favorite T.V. show. Now the decision is yours........

Once Vinci said: *Time stays long enough for those who use it.*

What do you think? The day had 48 hours for Leonardo? He used his maximum time and as result, he wrote more than 7000 pages covering so many fields and I will tell you somewhere in the book about his great works. He gave such paintings that made his name immortal.

So think about your interest, your special quality which no other has. I have the duty to make you great and successful. Don't leave it for too many smaller and not so important things and you will find yourself among great personalities of your city, nation or the world. The choice is whose? Just yours......

An average human looks without seeing, listens without hearing, touches without feeling, eats without tasting, and talks without thinking- Leonardo da Vinci

Do you prove anything wrong in the above statement? If yes, congrats!! You are more genius than Leonardo. If not, this is the right time to think for the right use of your right time in the right things. Always remember –

You will never have a greater or lesser dominion than that over yourself. The height of a man's success is gauged by his self-mastery; the depth of his failure by his self-abandonment. And this law is the expression of eternal justice. He who cannot establish dominion ever others.- Leonardo da Vinci

What can I say when everything is said by him. Accept your faults of not taking seriously your own interest, not making you great than what you are now.

Just discover the spark of success in yourself and I will tell you the path of success suggested by Leonardo da Vinci.

Are you ready guys???

Make Lists

Now we learned that every one of us can be successful but it is also true that getting success is not so easy to get easily. So we have to be organized and to do correct actions to achieve success.

The first and very important step is making a list of things to do. Make list for one day, for one year, and make a list of your goals to be achieved in your life. It must be time-bound. We can choose short-term goals and long-term goals separately.

Now let's see how Leonardo used this tool in his life. He used to make daily to-do lists. He always had a notebook with him. He wrote every question and every thought coming into his mind. I have managed to get one list from his notebook. Some things on that list are-

Find a master of hydraulics and get him to tell you how to repair a lock, canal, and mill in the Lombard manner.

Get Messer Friar (at the Benedictine Monastery to Milan) to show you De ponderibus (a medieval text on mechanics.

Describe the tongue of a woodpecker.

Think about what one will do with the description of a woodpecker. But this shows that he never missed a single thought what came to his mind. Due to this technique, he became the master of so many fields. One thing that is important to note that he not only made the lists but also did proper actions.

Scientific Theory

Now I will discuss with you the scientific theory of making lists. What is the psychological reason why some people love making to-do lists? And is there any fact that to-do lists make a person more effective?

Bluma Zeigarnik was the first psychologist who researched the psychology behind to-do lists. In 1927, she found in her study that people are more likely to remember unfinished tasks than finished ones, and interruptions during a task helped people to remain more detailed of the task itself. This is known as the Zeigarnik effect.

You can see the effect in action while in a bar or restaurant, where you forget delivered items but you remember clearly about the order undelivered. When that order gets delivered, you instantly forget it. Is this happen to you?

In 2011 psychologists E.J.Masieampo and R.F.Bameiser found that writing to-do lists can have a stilling and clear effect on our minds. Making to-do lists reduces the burden on the brain, which is struggling to hold a mental list of all the things we have to do. Releasing the burden of unfinished tasks on the mind frees it up to become more effective.

So what are you waiting for? Start making your to-do lists, as it is also proved by the science that if you write your goals, the chances of achieving them are more. Happy listing.

Most Important Mantra – Do Your Action

It is the most important and most known fact. Everyone knows that being successful is a result of doing an action in the right way. There is no shortcut to it.

I have been impressed with the urgency of doing. Knowing is not enough; We must apply. Being willing is not enough, we must do – Leonardo da Vinci

Leonardo knew the importance of doing. When he thought about the works of muscles in the human body. He decided to discover it. At his time, tempering with dead bodies was a serious criminal offense and the punishment for it was the death penalty. So he decided not to temper with dead bodies. Right??

No...... not at all. He used to visit graveyards to take dead bodies. He dissected more than 30 dead bodies, both deceased and healthy. As a result, he got a full understanding of the human body. Several people such as Plato and Aristotle had studied the topic before him, yet Vinci was among the first to provide both accurate drawings and explanations of the anatomy.

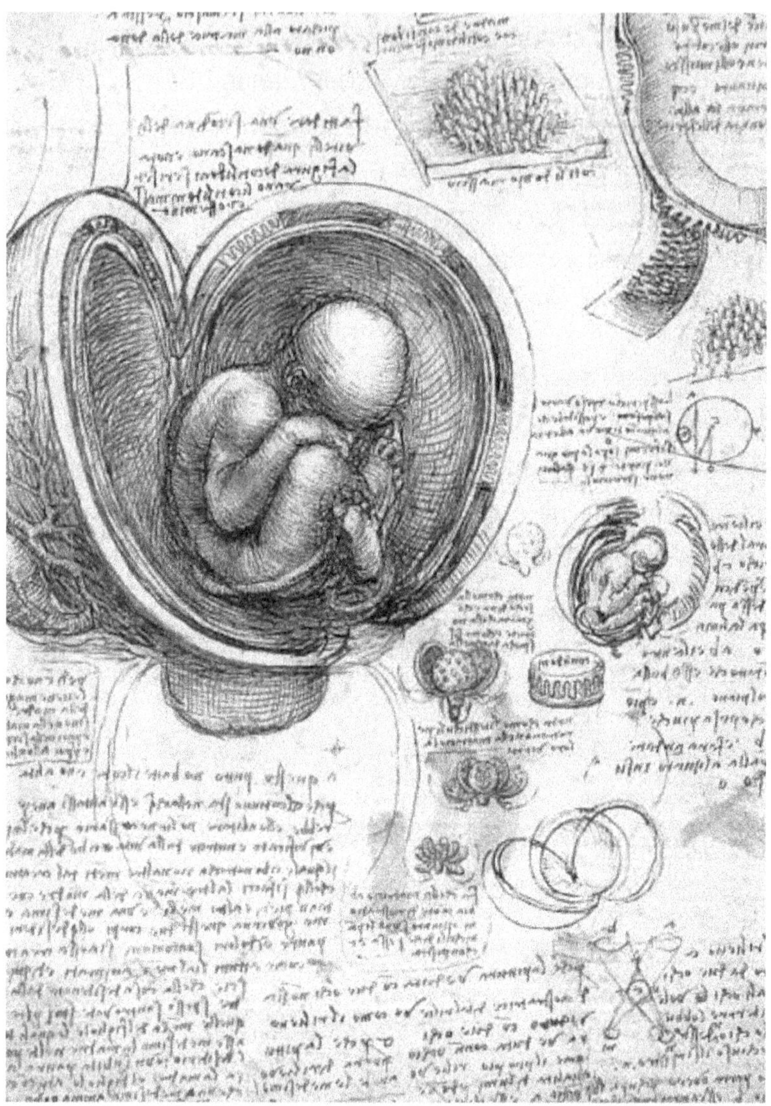

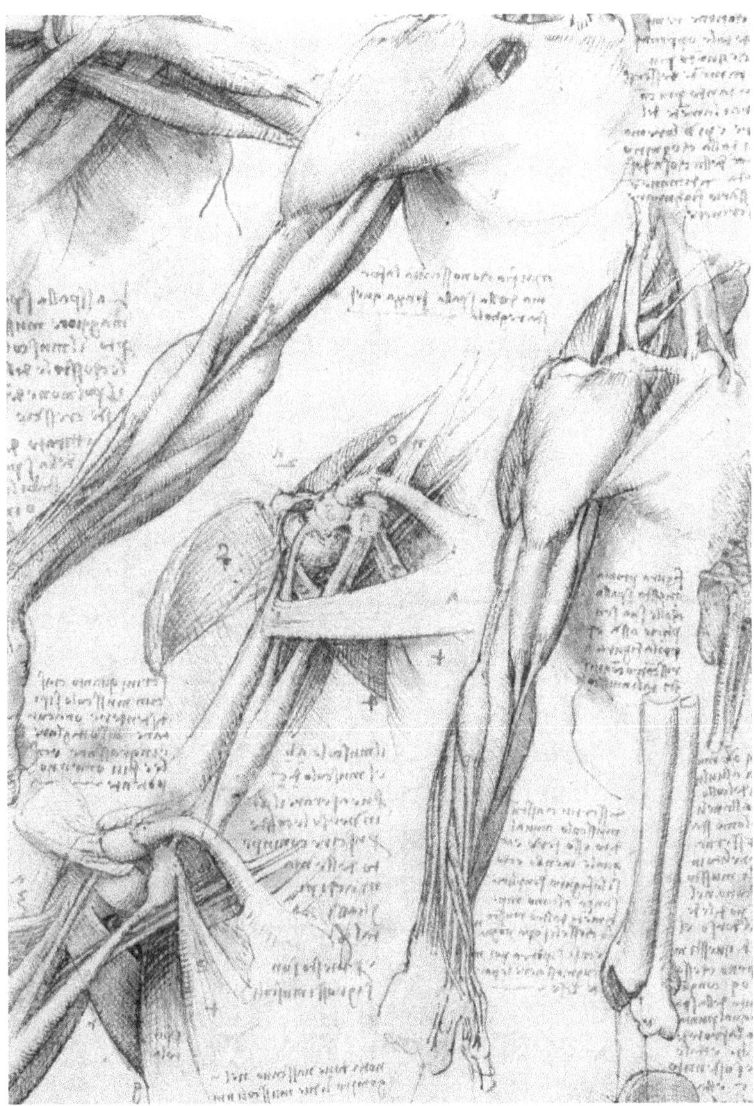

Unfortunately, no one took it seriously until the 1900s. Two notebooks of Leonardo were rediscovered in 1965. There are many sketches and devices, which led to the inventions and use of many medical methods used today. We will know later about his influence in the modern medical field in detail. Here I am giving some examples to know his greatness better.

The Surgical Robot:

One of the most famous things found in his notebook is a robot – Leonardo's robot. It was designed as a suit of armor that could stand, sit, wave its arms and raise its visor through a series of pulleys and machines. In 2002, Mark Rosheim built a prototype of Leonardo's robot and named as Robotic knight.

Leonardo's robot and his accurate sketches of the human anatomy inspired today's scientists to create a surgical robot. This surgical robot is named after da Vinci and is used today to perform many surgeries such as heart surgery, prostate surgery hysterectomies, and joint replacements.

Artificial Limbs and Synthetic Organs:

We see artificial limbs and synthetic organs. His studies on how limbs organs work have influenced scientists to create “replacements” for body parts in order for people to function normally.

Contact Lens:

Though contact lenses were not invented by Leonardo himself, he was the first to think up the idea of the contact lens. In 1508, da Vinci sketched the very first conceptual model of a contact lens, which contributed to the invention of the contact lens in 1808.

We all are wise enough to understand the need of doing actions. So act wisely for whatever your aim is. If we act with a purpose and if our manner is organized, we will get success surely.

Never Feel Distressed

I love those who can smile in trouble, who can gather strength from distress, and grow brave by reflection. ‘tis the business of little minds to shrink, but they whose art is firm, and whose conscience approves their conduct, will pursue their principles unto death.- Leonardo da Vinci

Success is not a cake to be digested in minutes. I believe, every one of us is the best creation of God or nature, whatever you believe. The aim of you must be something hard to achieve.

We can believe in ourselves or be convinced that everything depends upon fortune. I can't say, fortune has no role but no one can either be fortunate forever or be unfortunate till death. We have to try till our nose smells the success, not to be distressed or depressed.

Many of us believe that it is not possible to be unaffected by the major events of our life. But it is possible my dear. Let learn this lesson from da Vinci.

We know that Vinci lived far from his mother from the age of 5. His father was not able to give him, his much time. This cause is sufficient to make anyone depressed. Did Leonardo become depressed?

He lived alone most of his life. Did this reason make him sick?

He was never so rich, according to his talent but did he become disappointed?

Once he was charged with the crime of sodomy. He and some others were arrested when he was 24. The charges were not proved but that time phase was very difficult for him. It could make him distressed. Did he???

Not a single answer to the above question is in the affirmative. I gave these examples in front of you to prove only that you are not alone who faces difficulties.

Everyone has his unique type of difficulties which made his success unique.

Make your love for your goal so big that no hurdle takes you far from your great aim. Lit the fire of success within your heart and convert every hurdle into the fuel to maintain your fire.

Dreaming big is not a big deal. Anyone can do so but make your dream true by walking on the success path at every condition and tell me. I and you will celebrate your success with the world. Start your journey…….now.

As a well-spent day brings happy sleep, so life well used brings happy death- Leonardo da Vinci

Organized Manner of Doing Action

Your talent or idea is just like a child. You are the only person responsible for its birth. A baby never grows quickly. It takes a natural fixed time, so your ideas are. To nourish and to make it big is your own responsibility. Here we discuss step by step of doing actions for achieving something great. Here are the steps.

Taking the very first step

Taking the first step is usually the hardest part we have to do. Many of us want to be fit physically. We decide to go on a morning walk, doing yoga, or going to the gym from the very next morning. Many of did it so many times. Am I wrong?

What actually happens? we fail to rise early and after one or two attempts, we announce that we have no need of doing exercise, we are fit. In the case of an idea, we treat it in the same manner. If we are talking here about showing our talents, we do not try even once for it. Why?

The Fear of What if We Fail

Right?? Tell me one thing. What can be worse when you fail? The biggest failure is already with us, failure to show our unique talent, we have. Don't be fearful, just make your mind firm and start.

Make Regular Small Steps-

Many of us are strong enough in taking the first step. But 90% of us quit after a number of days. Why?

To find the answer, we have to know the influence of our minds. It wants relaxation. Our minds don't know the benefit of doing exercise. Wisdom has its office in the brain. Our mind knows the feeling. It feels pain and unrest in doing a new thing, so starts communicating with the brain and gives it thousands of reasons not to do that work. Poor brain!! The brain has only one reason to do but surrenders in front of thousands of reasons to quit and you know the result.

Psychologically, there are two terms agony and inertia. These two can be experienced before doing something risky. They take you out of your comfort zone. Either they make you stop or motivate you to take bigger steps. For example, you started your business and hope very next day a huge profit. Your enthusiasm fades after some days, and you quit that business. So never be trapped in mind games. If you understood the steps discussed in the book and take small but firm steps, you can achieve anything that you want. For practicing, your initial goals should be small. When you find success in smaller things, you will be confident and will achieve your big and real goal, for which you are living on the earth. So boost your enthusiasm and you will find yourself similar to a rocket.....

At last, just remember these points.

1. Take small steps regularly.
2. Don't try to jump in one big leap.

3. Don't be afraid to start small, all suppers are taken in pieces.
4. Don't try to do much at once.
5. Understand all the steps shown by da Vinci and start as early as possible.

Part Three

Some Works of Leonardo da Vinci

In the start, I said that Leonardo is the only Universal man of the earth till now. He was the master of more than 10 fields. Many of us know this fact but many don't know about it. To make you understand him more clearly, I am giving here some examples of his vast knowledge. Let us see some of his great works here.

In Paintings

Many of us know Leonardo's name only due to a great painting – MonaLisa. Maybe you know about the painting but not about Leonardo da Vinci. Leonardo started to paint this painting in 1503 but never ended it because he was never satisfied and always used to improve his work. Now it was an unfinished work according to the creator but it is the most expensive painting in the world. Just imagine the price of just a painting. Today the price of this painting is more than $ 860 million. If you want to see it, you can attend the Leonardo da Vinci exhibition at the Louvre Museum in Paris.

Who was MonaLisa

This is a very hot question till today. Some researchers believe that Leonardo made his own painting in the form of MonaLisa. Some believe that MonaLisa is nothing but the portrait of his own mother but the most voted and agreed point is that it is the painting of Lisa Gherardini, wife of Francesco Del Golconda. Francesco gave this project to Leonardo. He wanted this painting as the memory of the time of the second pregnancy of his wife. This painting is not so large as you can think. The measurement of this painting is just 30 inches by 21 inches and weighs 18 pounds.

Why so famous

Anyone can think, why this is painting so famous. This is due to the mysterious smile of

MonaLisa. The emotion of the smile changes when you change your direction of watching. You can see in the photograph of MonaLisa painting that there is a smile on her face but her eyes are looking sad. This is due to her pregnancy as many believe this is a normal thing in pregnancy. Oh yes, here I forgot to inform you that Leonardo took 12 years to paint this smile. Only 12 years!!! It can be a matter of surprise for us but nobody is Leonardo among us.

Some Interesting Facts

Napoleon and His Crush

The very famous and great emperor of France had MonaLisa hanging in his bedroom in the Tuileries Palace for about four years at the beginning of the 1800s. He was so fascinated with the painting due to his affection for a pretty Italian Teresa Guadagni. Now it is interesting that Teresa was a descendent of Lisa Gherardini, whose painting this is.

Eyebrows Missing

Sometimes we feel that something is missing in the painting. After carefully watching you can see that eyebrows are missing. Some claim that in the time of Leonardo, not keeping eyebrows was a fashion of the high class. Some claim that missing eyebrows are evidence that this masterpiece is unfinished. Now the interesting part is when scientists did ultra-detailed digital scans in 2007, they found that actually Leonardo painted the eyebrows but they simply faded over time.

Painting Receives Love Letters

There were more than one million artworks in Louvre Collection but MonaLisa alone received her own mail. She received a lot of love letters and the interesting part is that some of them were so ardent that this painting was kept under police protection.

Painting Has Been Attacked

This painting has been attacked several times. In 1956, a Bolivian, Ugo Ungaza Villegas chucked a rock at the portrait. A few months before one attacker threw acid at the painting. Due to these attacks, the left elbow part of the painting got damaged. So it was protected by bulletproof glass. Now the interesting part is that a Russian woman who had been denied French citizenship, threw a ceramic mug in 2009 at the painting to show her protest but due to bulletproof glass, the painting was safe.

There are a lot of interesting things about this and many other paintings painted by him but if you want I will share in another book as the topic of this book is different. Here I wanted to make you know about this painting. But I can tell you at last that many scientists are doing researches on it as there are many things to be researched about his all paintings. If you want to know more about it in detail, just tell me.

In Science

Aerial Screw (Helicopter)

We know that the first successful flight by any type of machine happened on Dec 17, 1903. The Wright brothers invented that, but the idea behind that invention was of George Cayley who thought it in 1799. But 600 years before this historical event, Leonardo gave many designs of flying man carrying objects. He designed a plane, a helicopter, and a parachute. It could be normal for some people but if you imagine yourself a person of the 14th century, these designs are more than sufficient to feel that Leonardo was a genius. He made himself thought several years ahead of his time.

Here I am telling about his designs of Aerial Screw. It is nearly the same as our helicopter. He drew this design in late 1480. When he was working as a military engineer from 1494 to 1499 posted by Ludovico Sforza, Duke of Milan.

The pen and ink sketch outlines a spiral rotor based on a water screw. The design comprises a solid circular platform, with a central vertical pole supported by three diagonal poles meeting at a small circular plane about halfway up the pole. The upper half of the pole is the supporting axis where a large spiraling sail of linen was fixed. To give it strength, the linen was stiffened with starch. When this linen aerial screw would push against the air with handles, the whole structure would lift into the air.

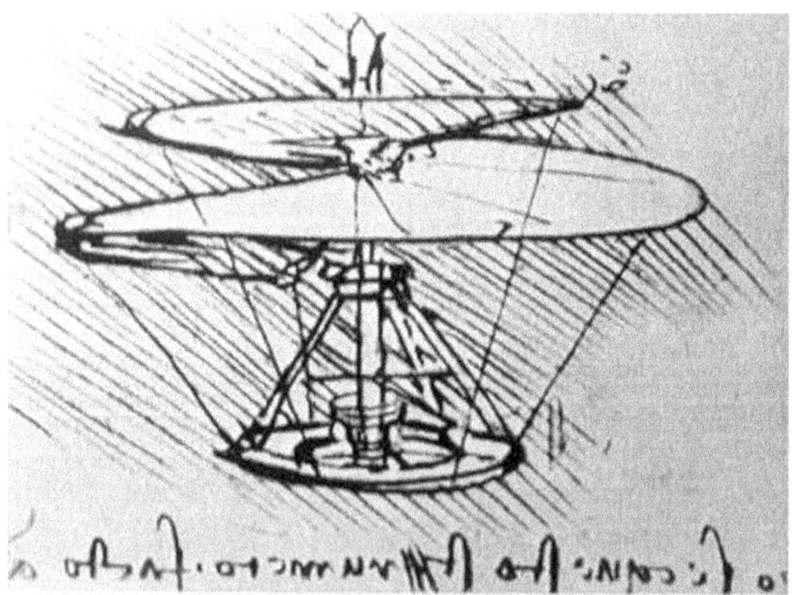

He made many small prototypes of it. Unfortunately, Duke of Milan was not interested in it so he dropped the idea of making it. What a professional helplessness this was.

Actually, he was the first who understood the basics of aerodynamics, yes it is true. He understood aerodynamics 600 years ago from now. He noted once in his notebook, which can be understood as 'it is the difference in pressure between the top and bottom of the wings which creates lift as the air flows over it.' Is this not the basic idea of modern aerodynamics? He also understood the wind tunnel principle and suggested that the aerodynamics properties of a body remain as same as they move through a medium at a given velocity.

I know that somewhere in your mind, you are accepting that Leonardo was a genius. He could be the father of aerodynamics but all his notes were decoded in later years. I strongly believe as many others believe that there are many designs of him to be understood for many inventions of the future.

Once anyone will surely make flying machines and man will be able to fly- Leonardo da Vinci

It becomes true after only 400 years.

Machine Guns

Vinci gave a concept of a machine gun cannon. He saw that cannons took a long time to reload. To counter this problem, he sketched a 33 barreled organ which has three rows of 11 guns each. In theory, one row would fire and left to be cooled and the third-row would load, so the soldiers could fire without interruption. Actually, the bronze cannon of the late 15th century closely resembled Vinci's design.

Refrigerators

Leonardo has all the capabilities to give us a shock. As he made an early prototype of a cooling machine also known as the refrigerator of today. His sketch shows an intricate system of ballows, leather chambers, and spouts that seem pretty bulky for something that doesn't keep all that much cool but it was designed in the 1400s. Vinci is known for doing the earliest attempt at refrigeration.

Parachutes

Vinci gave an early version of parachutes in his notebook 'The codex Atlanticus'. Just think that this man thought about so many things present today. His vision was made of sealed linen cloth and was held up by wooden poles. He never made it but had given the right idea. "If a man has a structure made out of a coated cloth 12 arms wide and 12 tall, he will be able to throw himself from any great height without hurting himself." Here you can see he used arms instead of meters because the meter was invented in 1793. Now you can understand that he gave these designs in which age of science.

Solar Power

Now you can tell me that using solar power is a modern phenomenon, but that's not true. Leonardo da Vinci designed his solar power system to heat water for Florence. He experimented and predicted that concave reflective mirrors could be used to focus sunlight and harness it.

In Geology

When scientific pioneers around 1800 recognized fossils for what they are – traces of ancient animals- and analyzed the processes that create and erode rocks, they quickly reached a set of conclusions that led to Darwin's theory of evolution but Leonardo thought a lot of key discoveries hundreds of years ago.

He had the following amazing insights about geology and fossils:

1. Shells that appear on mountain tops and fish bones in caves must be the remains of animals that long ago swam in these places when they were covered in the sea. The claims that they were swept there by the biblical flood is a completely inadequate explanation. So the surface of the earth has changed over time, with the land where once there was a sea.
2. The most powerful natural force is the movement of water in rivers. Water has sculpted the very largest features of the landscape, a process that must have taken a landscape, a process that must have taken a very long time.
3. Therefore slow and relentless natural processes, not the divine instantaneous act described in Genesis, have shaped our planet.

These were not only his thoughts. He did actual research. When he lived in the court of Duke of Milan, he was closed to the Alps. He went walking in the mountains and climbed to the top of Monte Rosa. He wrote in his notes about exploring a mountain cave where he found massive fossil bones. And revealed that he was famous for this interest in rocks and strange forms hidden within them.

> Centuries later, Leonardo's recognition that fossils tell the story of the Earth would be rediscovered by science and this insight would overturn religious views of creation.

On the Flights of Birds

Leonardo studied and watched deeply the flights of birds. He dissected many birds too to understand the basics of their body design. He wrote a book in 1505 about the flight of birds. The name of this book is 'Codex on the Flight of Birds'. It comprises 18 folios. At present, you can see his original book at the Royal Library of Turin.

In this codex, Leonardo was the first who used the terms center of gravity and center of pressure. Is it not surprising?

Here I will share some basic points of this book only. In folio 1, he is telling about the relation of density and weight. He asks that why ice floats in water if it is the denser of the two. Today this could be a normal question but we must remember his time frame. On the last page of this folio, he explains why an object falling down the arc of a curve will fall faster than the object falls down the chord of a curve. He explains that the angle of a chord is half of the angle of the curve makes between the midpoint, endpoint, and horizontal, and since this angle is half then the speed will also be half. He compares this with an angle of the arc and tells that an object falling down an arc will be 7/8 faster than if were to fall down the chord of a curve. I always become very surprised when I read about his works. How one could be so genius!!

At one place of folio 2, he says that if a balance is suspended in its center of gravity, then it would not move or oscillate, regardless of position.

In folio 5, he says that a bird that is going in a straight line that comes into a cross breeze at a perpendicular angle will now be heading in a direction that is in between the two endpoints of each direction. He explains if a bird in a descent wants to turn left or right, then it will lower the wing on the side of the direction it wants to turn.

Here I am telling about his notes about how to fly a machine like a bird. Here are his instructions.

Situation	Note
Wingtip is turned towards the wind	This wing must be put above or below the wind along with the side of the tail and the rudder of the wing's humorous.
While descending	The side nearest to the center of gravity will descend first.
While descending	The heavier part of the machine will be in front of the geometric center.
While descending	The heavier part of the machine will never be equal to or higher than the lighter part.
While stably flying	If the resistance from the wing is moved behind the center of gravity, the machine will descend head first.
While descending	If the tail rotates backward, the

tail first	machine will regain balance. If the tail rotates forward, the machine will flip over.
While stably flying	If the resistance from the wing is moved in front of the center of gravity, the machine will descend first.

So you can see how carefully and deeply he studied whatever he studied. I wrote all these to make you understand that Leonardo was a true genius and what we learn from him can make us successful in every field whatever we want. So be serious about your goal and do whatever you learned from this book and no one can stop you from achieving success in your life. Be successful ....

What You Want

Hope you like the book. You can share your thought about the book with me. You can mail me at 1972ji@gmail.com or visit the website

Here I want to know your opinion about what you want to read next. Here is the list of books of e Leonardo da Vinci series. What you tell will be published first. So share your thoughts.

1. The Mysteries of Leonardo's Paintings
2. Science and Leonardo da Vinci
3. Leonardo da Vinci and human anatomy

www.ingramcontent.com/pod-product-compliance
Ingram Content Group UK Ltd.
Pitfield, Milton Keynes, MK11 3LW, UK
UKHW022007190726
13853UKWH00004B/1786